NARROW GAUGE
RAILWAYS OF SAXONY

JOHN WOODHAMS

AMBERLEY

First published 2023

Amberley Publishing
The Hill, Stroud,
Gloucestershire, GL5 4EP

www.amberley-books.com

ISBN: 978 1 3981 0814 1 (print)
ISBN: 978 1 3981 0815 8 (ebook)

British Library Cataloguing in Publication Data.
A catalogue record for this book is available from the British Library.

Typeset in 10pt on 13pt Celeste.
Typesetting by SJmagic DESIGN SERVICES, India.
Printed in Great Britain.

Contents

THE RAILWAYS OF SAXONY

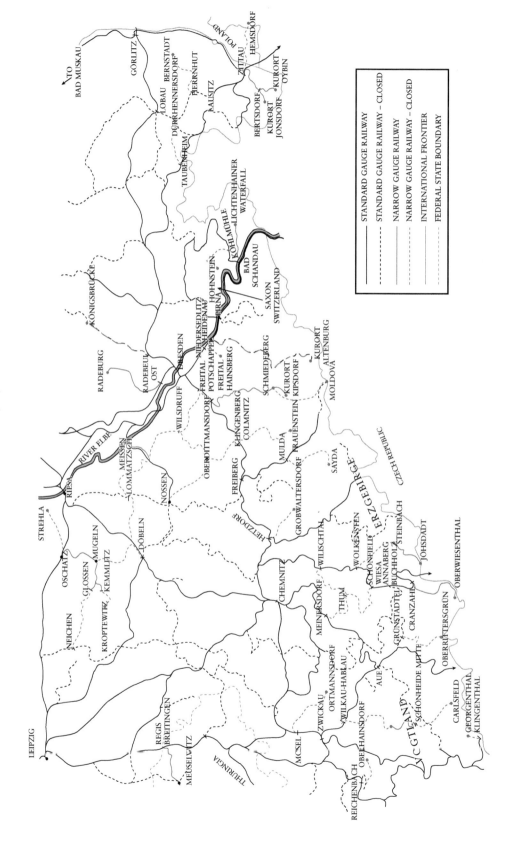

Legend:
- STANDARD GAUGE RAILWAY
- STANDARD GAUGE RAILWAY – CLOSED
- NARROW GAUGE RAILWAY
- NARROW GAUGE RAILWAY – CLOSED
- INTERNATIONAL FRONTIER
- FEDERAL STATE BOUNDARY

TO BAD MUSKAU

POLAND

HEMSDORF
ZITTAU
KURORT OYBIN
KURORT JONSDORF
BERTSDORF
LAUSITZ
HERRNHUT
BERNSTADT
DÜRRHENNERSDORF
LÖBAU
GÖRLITZ
TAUBENHEIM

KÖNIGSBRÜCKE
RADEBURG
RADEBEUL OST
DRESDEN
NIEDERSEDLITZ
HEIDENAU
PIRNA
HOHNSTEIN
KOHLMÜHLE
LICHTENHAINER WATERFALL
BAD SCHANDAU
SAXON SWITZERLAND

RIESA
STREHLA
MEISSEN
LOMMATZSCH
NOSSEN
WILSDRUFF
FREITAL POTSCHAPPEL
FREITAL HAINSBERG
KLINGENBERG COLMNITZ
SCHMIEDEBERG
KURORT KIPSDORF
KURORT ALTENBURG
MOLDOVA
OBERDITTMANNSDORF
FREIBERG
MULDA
FRAUENSTEIN
GROßWALTERSDORF
SAYDA
HETZDORF

RIVER ELBE

OSCHATZ
MÜGELN
GLOSSEN
KEMMLITZ
NEICHEN
KROPTEWITZ
DÖBELN
CHEMNITZ
MEINERSDORF
THUM
WILLISCHTAL
WOLKENSTEIN
SCHÖNFELD
WIESA
ANNABERG
BUCHHOLZ
STEINBACH
JÖHSTADT
CZECH REPUBLIC
ERZGEBIRGE
OBERWIESENTHAL
CRANZAHL
GRÜNSTÄDTEL
SCHÖNHEIDE MITTE
OBERRITTERSGRÜN
CARLSFELD
GEORGENTHAL
KLINGENTHAL
AUE
ORTMANNSDORF
WILKAU-HASLAU
ZWICKAU
OBERHAINSDORF
VOGTLAND
MOSEL
REICHENBACH
MEUSELWITZ
REGIS BREITINGEN
LEIPZIG
THURINGIA

1

The Development of the Saxon State Railways Narrow Gauge

The state of Saxony lies in eastern Germany, bordering Poland to the east, and the Czech Republic to the south. Most of the terrain is hilly and mountainous, chiefly comprising the Erzgebirge, or Ore Mountains, which stretch for around 160 kilometres along the southern edge and rise to some 1,200 metres. The hills to the south-west are a region known as Oberes Vogtland or Upper Vogtland, while to the north-east lie the Lausitz hills. The capital city of Dresden is situated on the River Elbe, and much of the river south of the city towards the Czech border offers dramatic scenery, the area being known as 'Saxon Switzerland'. The North German Plain extends into the area surrounding Leipzig in the northern part of the state.

The very name Ore Mountains is suggestive of mineral deposits, and that is indeed so, with a long history of mining gold, silver, lead, tungsten and more recently uranium, although this too has ceased. Lignite, or brown coal, is still mined in the area around Leipzig.

The two main cities of Dresden and Leipzig were linked by a privately financed standard gauge railway in 1839, but most subsequent developments were either promoted or supported by the state, although there were privately owned coal railways around Zwickau when in 1869 the Royal General Division of the Saxon State Railways, or Königlich Generaldirektion der Sächsische Staatseisenbahnen, was formed.

By the early 1870s, the main railway network had been completed, linking most of the main towns and cities. Although a standard gauge railway running north to south through the Erzgebirge via Annaberg-Buchholz had been built, the prohibitive costs of construction in such hilly terrain, linking smaller towns and villages, precluded further expansion.

In 1864, a private proposal had been put forward to build a narrow gauge railway from Wilkau, south of Zwickau, to Kirchberg, where the growing local textile industry, reliant on local water power, realised that a railway would provide access to coal supplies and aid expansion. However, it was not until 1876 that another scheme was actually put before Parliament. Despite a royal decree of November 1877, the Saxon Parliament did not support the narrow gauge proposal, despite the much lower costs of construction.

Two years later another decree put forward more proposals, including a line from Oschatz to Mügeln and Döbeln, plus another from Freital-Hainsberg to Schmiedeberg.

There was a further submission for a line from Leipzig to Geithain, which was in fact subsequently built as a standard gauge line.

The Wilkau–Kirchberg railway finally gained the support of Parliament in March 1880, and construction work commenced in May 1881. Because expensive earthworks had been minimised, with the line largely following an existing road, the opening ceremony was held less than six months later on 16 October, with services commencing the following day. The advantages of a 750-mm narrow gauge railway became clear to members of Parliament the following month when they were invited to visit the railway by the state's Finance Minister.

A 4-kilometre extension to Saupersdorf was started almost immediately, although this was a more expensive stretch, which required considerable engineering works and finally opened on 30 November 1882.

Meanwhile, construction was also underway on a second line south-west of Dresden, the 26-kilometre Weisseritztalbahn from Freital-Hainsberg to the resort of Kurort Kipsdorf. The line largely followed the valley of the Rote Weisseritz river, hence its name, with the route from Freital to Schmiedeberg being opened on 1 November 1882, and the final section to Kipsdorf following on 3 September the following year.

At Oschatz, a town on the main line midway between Dresden and Leipzig, the narrow gauge line southwards via Mügeln to Döbeln was opened in 1884. Another line from Mügeln via Nebitzschen to Neichen followed four years later. Mügeln was to become the hub of an extensive network, with the final route, an extension from Döbeln to Lommatzsch, completed in 1911.

An extension from Oschatz to Strehla was opened in 1891, and that line was built principally to provide access to a quayside and loading facilities on the River Elbe. Kaolin traffic from a mine at Kemmlitz could then be carried in narrow gauge wagons direct to the quay.

Opened in October 1881, Kirchberg was the terminus of the first narrow gauge line in Saxony, until the further extension to Carlsfeld was completed. (Traditionsbahn Radebeul)

A view of the original terminus station at Kurort Kipsdorf, opened in 1883.

The branch from Oschatz to Strehla commenced operation in 1891, initially using Saxon I K class locomotives.

Another mini-network was established centred around Thum, the first 14-kilometre section between Wilischtal and Thum opening in December 1886. The next line, from Schonfeld to Thum via Tannenberg and Geyer, involved the construction of a large steel viaduct, the 180-metre-long Greifenbachtal Brücke, which could claim to be one of the largest narrow gauge structures built in Germany. With the arrival of the second line in 1906 a new, more convenient junction station was built at Thum. In 1911, another line was opened from Thum to Meinersdorf, a station on the main line between Chemnitz and Aue.

A line was also built from Mosel along the valley of the Zwickauer Mulde to Ortmannsdorf. The inaugural train on the opening day disgraced itself by derailing en route at Mulsen St Jacob, and with the very rural nature of the route it was never successful financially.

One further group of lines developed, known as the Wilsdruffer Netz, taking its name from the town that became a junction at its heart. The first part of this network was a line from Freital Potschappel (with a link to the then existing line at Freital-Hainsberg) via Wilsdruff to Nossen. At Potschappel the route was shared with a standard gauge railway that served the coal industry at Niederhermsdorf (later named Wurgwitz), resulting in mixed gauge track for some 2 kilometres. In 1901, a freight train was completely blown off the embankment approach to Kesselsdorf Bridge due to strong winds, but fortunately without injury. A separate, isolated line was then built from Klingenthal, a station on the Dresden to Chemnitz main line, southwards to Frauenstein. It was not until 1909 that another railway was constructed from Wilsdruff to Meissen and finally, as late as 1923, the last stretch from Klingenthal to Oberdittmannsdorf was opened.

Oberrittersgrün station *c.* 1890 with Saxon I K and train. (Oberrittersgrün Museum collection)

The locomotive shed at Wilsdruff under construction in 1894. (M. Rost)

A similar view shortly after opening in 1895. (M. Rost)

Station staff pose for the camera at Wilsdruff in 1912.

A 1901 view of Grumbach station, situated on the line between Freital Potschappel and Wilsdruff.

The scene of the accident at Kesselsdorf in 1901, when strong winds blew an entire train off bridge and embankment.

A Class IV K locomotive stands at Mohorn station, between Wilsdruff and Nossen, *c.* 1905, with a train of both bogie and four-wheel stock.

At Zittau, in the south-eastern corner of the state, a line was built to Reichenau and Markersdorf, which opened in November 1884. A treaty between the state of Saxony and what was then Austria-Hungary in 1898 envisaged the extension of the line to a border station at Hemsdorf, linking with the Friedland District Railway in Bohemia. The short extension to Hemsdorf opened in 1900, but while the treaty had stipulated that there should be two cross-border through trains in each direction daily, this never actually happened, and passengers always had to change at Hemsdorf.

Several prominent business people in Zittau started to campaign for the construction of a railway to the resorts of Kurort Oybin and Kurort Jonsdorf, but Saxon State Railways were not interested in the scheme. Undeterred, they raised sufficient finance to promote and build the line themselves and on 28 March 1889 the Zittau Oybin Jonsdorf Eisenbahn Gesellschaft was granted permission to go ahead. The construction period was stipulated not to exceed eighteen months, and that the specification should comply with the state railways own lines. The state also retained the right to nationalise if it so chose. The new line branched off the Reichenau route, running to Bertsdorf, a junction station for the two branches to Oybin and Jonsdorf. The opening ceremony on 25 November 1890 was marred by storm damage, and trains could only operate to Bertsdorf. The railway remained in private hands until becoming part of the national network in 1906. At its opening the railway possessed just seven four-wheel carriages, but traffic levels were such that another ten were required by the following year.

There were also plans to extend the Wilkau–Kirchberg line southwards to Schönheide and ultimately Carlsfeld. The extension to Schönheide was approved in 1890, but it proved to be a difficult and relatively expensive route with problems caused by marshy ground

A general view of Carlsfeld. This southern terminus of the line from Wilkau-Hasslau was not reached until 1897.

conditions, and the requirement for three substantial viaducts, including that across the Zwickauer Mulde, a steel structure 187 metres long and 34 metres high. Several other bridges were built using unreinforced concrete.

The further extension to Carlsfeld also proved difficult. Although narrow gauge railways could be built relatively cheaply, often following river valleys and existing roads, this could involve some very tight curves to minimise expense. Equally, there were some fairly steeply graded sections, with one 700-metre stretch of the line between Schönheide and Carlsfeld at a grade of 1 in 20 – the steepest section of any of the lines described here. The final section of the railway opened in June 1897 – the transport link that the local glassmaking and woodworking industries had campaiged for had at last arrived. In 1903, a serious accident occurred near Rothenkirchen, with some carriages and the locomotive ending up on their sides. The cause was found to be excessive speed.

Three further lines were built in the Dresden area, all of which survive today: one with steam operation, and the other two converted to standard gauge and worked as modern branch lines. The route from Radebeul Ost via Moritzburg to Radeburg was opened in September 1884, while the Müglitztalbahn, from Mügeln bei Pirna (which is now part of Heidenau) to Geising followed in 1890. This steeply graded line served the forestry industry along the river valley, plus the watchmaking factories at Glashütte, but only a few years after opening was severely damaged in the floods of 1897. A narrow gauge line from Klotzsche, north-east of the city to Königsbrück, was opened in October 1884. Such was the increase in volume of traffic over the next few years, coupled with the building of a new military complex at Königsbrück, that it was decided to convert the line to standard gauge as early as 1896. Much of the work was done with the line still open, and the rebuilt line was commissioned in April the following year.

Another accident two years later, at Rothenkirchen, resulted in the locomotive resting on its side.

In Saxon Switzerland a new line was built from Köhlmühle along the Schwarzbach Valley to Hohnstein, and opened in 1897. This was a much more rural railway with little industry en route.

Various proposals were put forward for a railway to the Fichtelberg mountain and the town of Oberwiesenthal, from a junction on the standard gauge railway between Annaberg Buchholz and Weipert. Eventually Cranzahl was the choice of junction, and although the line was set out in 1894 it only opened late in 1897, the difficult route resulting in a much more expensive line than intended. However, it allowed the town of Oberwiesenthal, once a centre of silver mining, to develop as a summer and winter resort.

Part of the route between Freital-Hainsberg and Kurort Kipsdorf was rerouted between 1907 and 1912 to allow for the construction of Malter Dam, and its associated reservoir.

It was very soon realised that transhipping freight between narrow gauge and standard gauge wagons was an inefficient and expensive process, which could be eliminated if goods could be transported in standard gauge stock throughout.

A container system was introduced at Klotzsche, whereby bodies were lifted off standard gauge wagons and on to narrow gauge stock, but this facility soon became redundant with the line's conversion to standard gauge. Alternative methods were used on other lines, with complete vehicles carried either on transporter wagons, *rollwagen*, or small trollies or trailers clamped to each axle, known as *rollböcke*. The use of both became widespread, but it was of course necessary for the narrow gauge lines to have a suitably large and generous loading gauge to handle such traffic, plus locomotives powerful enough for heavier trains.

A carefully posed image of Hohnstein, terminus of the Schwarzbachbahn, in 1907. (Schwarzbachbahn collection)

A general view of Frauenstein, terminus of the line from Klingenberg to Colmnitz, opened in 1898.

Gruß aus dem Erzgebirge.

Bahnhof Sayda.

Sayda station, the terminus of the line from Mulda, opened in 1897 and closed to traffic in 1966.

The building of the narrow gauge railways had certainly allowed the development of a variety of industries, and improved both freight and passenger transport links for many smaller towns and villages, particularly those in areas with difficult hilly terrain. Journey times were invariably fairly relaxed, but the lines were proving to be a valuable resource even if they, in themselves, were barely profitable, if at all.

At Glashütte, in the Müglitz Valley, a Class IV K Saxon Meyer locomotive waits with its train, *c.* 1910.

A train approaches Thum station, around 1910.

Shortly after arrival at Kurort Kipsdorf in 1909 train crew and station staff pose for the photographer. (Traditionsbahn Radebeul)

A double-ended Class II K locomotive heads a train at Schmiedeberg on 1 May 1891. (Bernd Hauptvogel)

Bernstadt station opened in 1893, the terminus of the line from Herrnhut, but was an early casualty, closing in 1945. (Traditionsbahn Radebeul)

An 0-6-0T Class I K leads a train near Thurm, on the line between Mosel and Ortmannsdorf. (Traditionsbahn Radebeul)

Two World Wars and the Reichsbahn Takeover 1914–45

By the outbreak of the First World War the Saxon narrow gauge network was largely complete, but there were still schemes at the planning stage. The existing line from Heidenau to Gleising terminated some 3 kilometres short of the original intended destination at Altenberg (although the upper station had optimistically been named Gleising-Altenberg). Although the campaign to extend the line was initially unsuccessful, the construction was implemented as a government project after the Armistice in 1918, and opened on 10 November 1923. Other schemes were proposed to extend the line still further to link with the Weisseritztalbahn at Kurort Kipsdorf, or alternatively Moldova or Frauenstein, but additional expenditure could not be justified.

Another scheme was planned for a line from Schmiedeberg, a station on the Kipsdorf line, along the Pöbel Valley to link with a standard gauge line at Moldova. Construction of the proposed Pöbeltalbahn was started in March 1920, and nearly 10 kilometres of railway was built before the project was abandoned in 1923, although the unfinished right of way was retained until the 1960s.

The railways were only indirectly affected by the First World War, the main issues resulting from loss of staff to the war effort, and demands from the military for locomotives and equipment, plus shortage of some materials, particularly as the conflict wore on.

In April 1920 the Saxon State Railways had become part of a new company, Deutsche Reichseisenbahn, (German Imperial railways), which was established by the Weimar government. This state-owned concern became more simply Deutsche Reichsbahn in 1924.

Although the government had committed funds to extend the Müglitz Valley line to Altenberg, demands from industries in the valley to increase the capacity of the railway, which was becoming increasingly busy, were not heeded. Four years after the extension opened, in 1927, the line was badly damaged by flooding. Meanwhile, a new source of freight traffic had been found – ice from a lake near Altenberg to customers in Dresden. The increase in traffic levels was such that in 1934 Deutsche Reichsbahn

A busy scene at Kurort Kipsdorf during the winter sporting season of 1920.

A train crosses the viaduct over the Sebnitzbach and approaches Schwarzberg Tunnel in 1926. (Schwarzbachbahn collection)

decided to convert the line to standard gauge. The easing of curves and the general redesign of much of the line meant that the rebuilt line was nearly 2 kilometres shorter. When the line reopened in December 1938 journey times had been considerably reduced too.

By the 1930s the Weisseritztalbahn was also enjoying an increase in excursion traffic not only to the resort of Kipsdorf, but also along the route to Rabenau, and the newly constructed Malter Dam. Between 1932 and 1934 the upper terminus was remodelled and extended with four platform roads, plus signalling systems were also modernised and improved both here and at the Zittau lines. In the previous decade the section between Obercarsdorf and Buschmühle, just below Kipsdorf, had been rerouted, resulting in the construction of a new viaduct at Schmiedeberg.

On many other lines passenger traffic was fairly sparse, and expansion of the rural bus network in the 1920s eroded that traffic further. Costs were escalating with a period of hyperinflation, and the introduction of an eight-hour working day wreaking havoc in the economy. The competing bus routes were often provided by the Saxon state's own operator, or the Reichspost. Despite the primitive state of many roads, they were often able to offer shorter journey times and not unattractive fares. Many railways also carried mail traffic, with special carriages for post, but by the mid-1930s the transfer of that traffic to road had also started, although much of it returned to the railway for the duration of the Second World War. While Oybin and Jonsdorf were served by up to ten trains daily, many other routes only saw two or three passenger trains in each direction daily, for example Wolkenstein to Jöhstadt, and Döbeln to Lommatzsch.

The castle dominates this 1924 view of a train leaving Bärenstein, in the Müglitz Valley.

Flooding devastated the Müglitz Valley in 1927, wrecking Glashütte station and rolling stock.

This view of Glashütte one year later gives no indication of the earlier destruction.

A general view of the terminus at Kurort Kipsdorf following the remodelling of the early 1930s.

The spacious concours area of the new booking hall, with stairs leading down to platform level.

Würgwitz, on the line between Freital Potschappel and Wilsdruff, was the scene of an accident in November 1935, when the steel viaduct collapsed under a passing double headed freight train. While the leading pilot engine remained on a more or less undamaged part of the trestle structure, the train engine was less lucky, becoming entangled in the wreckage of the bridge. The line was repaired and operational again two months later. The accident occurred despite the fact that some ten years earlier the line had been substantially upgraded and strengthened to accept the heavier Class VI K locomotives involved.

The railways largely escaped damage during the Second World War, but as in the previous conflict suffered from staff being drawn into the Wehrmacht. The armaments industry throughout Germany was decentralised, and many smaller factories in the communities served by the narrow gauge were turned over to the war effort. This could mean additional freight traffic, and also in some cases a huge rise in commuter traffic. For example, the Taubenheim–Dürrennersdorf line served a Siemens factory, which led to over 1,000 new commuters daily. Textile works along the Wilkau–Carlsfeld line were also adapted for arms production, and the importance of the railway was such that it was completely relaid between 1939 and 1944, but, as a sign of the times, with forced Czech labour.

The Schönfeld Wiesa–Meinersdof route served several aircraft factories, and towards the end of the conflict a locomotive on the line was damaged by an air attack, and the railway at Lommatzsch also suffered track damage.

As the end approached, and the fronts became closer, the railways simply stopped running, and in several instances the Wehrmacht blew up bridges against the advancing forces.

3

Behind the Iron Curtain
1945–90

The railways emerged from the Second World War in a thoroughly run-down condition, with the major railway workshops in the region suffering from severe damage too. At the end of the war, the greater part of Saxony was occupied by the Soviet Union, while initially the south-western area, part of the Vogtland region, had been captured by the Americans and remained temporarily under their control until June 1945. For a time, one area remained unoccupied by Allied troops and became known as the Free State of Schwarzenberg. Eventually the entire state was part of the Soviet zone and, with the subsequent division of Germany, found itself part of the communist-led Deutsche Demokratische Republik, or German Democratic Republic (GDR).

The German/Polish border had now been moved westwards, and most of the line from Zittau via Reichenau to Hemsdorf found itself in the new Poland, with Hemsdorf itself now in Czechoslovakia. The last traffic across the old border at Hemsdorf ran on 2 May 1945, with the last train to Reichenau on 22 June. Hemsdorf now became Hermanice and Bogatynia the new name for Reichenau. The new frontier was just to the east of Zittau, at the River Neisse, or Nysa. In 1951, the line from Sienawka, formerly Kleinschönau, on the Polish side of the river border, to Bogatynia/Reichenau was reopened, with a new narrow gauge extension to Turoszow. This new line was converted to standard gauge in 1960 to serve a new opencast coal mine at Bogatynia, and the old narrow gauge line was abandoned shortly afterwards. The Czech part of the line, at Hermanice, was closed in 1947, but reopened a few years later to serve a quarry. Passenger services resumed in 1958 and continued until 1976, by which time the stone quarry traffic had long ceased. The track, however, remained in situ for another twenty years.

A few days before the end of the war, the Wehrmacht destroyed the viaduct close to Dürrennersdorf on the line from Taubenheim. Although trains were running again a month later, it was only a short reprieve as the line closed completely in September. The Pliessnitztalbahn, which ran from Herrnhut to Bernstadt, also ceased operation on 2 October 1945, and the track of both railways was immediately dismantled and removed together with rolling stock and locomotives by the Soviet Union as war reparations.

Intriguingly, the Bernstadt line still appeared on railway maps over twenty years later as a 'railway without track'.

In May 1945, the railway between Mosel and Ortmannsdorf initially found itself split between the two zones of allied occupation, and, although the last passenger train had run in 1939, the line continued with freight working until it closed abruptly in May 1951. The Schwarzbachbahn from Kohlmühle to Hohnstein also closed just a week later, and both railways were promptly dismantled and the recovered materials and equipment taken to Berlin for use in the construction of the 'Berlin Ring', a new main line railway, 125 kilometres in length, built by the GDR government to bypass West Berlin.

The shortage of serviceable locomotives and rolling stock resulted in such a drastically reduced level of service that in 1947 a total of 467 passenger carriages, out of a total of 521, were stored out of use. This situation was not entirely resolved until the middle of the following decade with a programme of locomotive building.

Although uranium had been discovered in the Erzgebirge mountains many years earlier, the Soviet Union, which in the first years of the occupying powers had control of the region, sought to exploit the resource in its bid to develop atomic weapons, retaining a very strong influence after the division of Germany and the formation of the new GDR government. The mining company Wismut AG was directly controlled by the NKVD, later to become the KGB, which established exclusion zones and strict security around its areas of operation. One such location was the town of Aue, where special passes were required, which resulted in restrictions on the narrow gauge line between Wilkau and Carlsfeld. This line had been unable to operate properly since 1945 as a viaduct had been deliberately destroyed at Wilzschaus, severing the line, and only one locomotive was operational on the northern section. Later, in 1954, a 2-kilometre section of the line was badly damaged by flooding. However, the uranium mining brought additional traffic not only to this railway, but to the Pöhlwassertalbahn as well, between Grünstädtel and Oberritersgrün.

The Cranzahl–Oberwiesenthal line, which had always relied heavily on tourist traffic, was only running intermittently at the end of the war, and although it was initially in an unoccupied zone, by 1947 the area was declared a restricted area and the railway was called upon to remove ore extracted from the Bärenstein mine and transport up to 3,000 workers to and from the mine daily. Winter sports and other tourist traffic was only permitted from 1955 when the access restrictions were eased. Another uranium mine was planned close to the Mulda–Sayda route, but this was not developed and therefore the anticipated extra freight traffic did not materialise.

The little railways continued to serve local industries, carrying a wide range of freight, from refrigerators and fire appliances on the Pressnitztalbahn to serving ironworks, paper mills and even the broom factory at Stützengrün. The remaining lines soldiered on, but by the early 1960s it was clear that major investment in track renewals, and new or overhauled locomotives and rolling stock was urgently needed, but set against gradually declining traffic levels, both passenger and freight. The government commissioned a study into the future of the narrow gauge, which concluded that the expenditure required to keep them operational either as steam-operated lines or with new diesel locomotives could not be justified, and furthermore suitable diesel replacements were simply not available. On 14 May 1964 it was announced that all lines would close by 1975. In the meantime, the works at Görlitz were busy rebuilding older Meyer IV K locomotives, described in more detail in Chapter 5.

This inevitably led to a howl of protests, with claims that suitable replacement bus services, and facilities for road haulage were either not available or fit for purpose. The line from Mügeln to Döbeln lost its passenger service almost immediately in December 1964, though it remained open for freight for another three years. Similarly, the line from Lommatzsch to Meissen was closed to passenger traffic in 1966, but the section from Löthain to Lommatzsch carried freight until 1972. For the last two years of operation it was an isolated stretch following the closure of the link from Lommatzsch to Döbeln in 1970. Although only seasonal, sugar beet was an important source of freight revenue on the lines serving Döbeln beet factory, and this traffic survived to the end.

The round of closures in the late 1960s attracted quite a lot of attention with last train farewells and protests, not unlike the Beeching era closures in the UK. This led the authorities to announce further closures at very short notice. By the end of 1972 the only part of the Mügeln network that was still working was the Oschatz–Kemmlitz section – it still survives today. The Thumer network was reduced to the section between Thum and Meinersdorf, but that too had gone by 1974.

Freight traffic ended on the line between Mulda and Sayda in July 1966, but passenger traffic continued for a few more weeks until complete closure. The line had enjoyed considerable excursion traffic throughout the 1950s and into the early 1960s, and the lack of a suitable alternative bus service had provided other regular traffic, but ultimately the decline was not enough to save the railway. Although track removal commenced in 1967, it was interrupted by the military build up around the Prague Spring in summer 1968, and not completed until the end of that year. The steelwork from the Muldenthal Viaduct was removed, but the stone pillars remained, and have now been preserved.

Many lines were closed in the 1970s, and on 27 May 1972 the last train between Thum and Wilischtal crosses the Zschopaubrücke.

Another view of the last train to Wilischtal – note the coupling extension pole, for use with standard gauge *rollwagen*, resting on the trestles. (H. Leckmeier)

The halt at Venusberg Spinnerei is showing signs of decay and neglect during the final days of operation. (H. Leckmeier)

Closure of the Pöhlwassertalbahn to Oberrittersgrün was originally planned for 1969, but again a lack of suitable replacement bus services meant that the trains continued to run until September 1971, with the track removed over the next two years. However, it was not all removed, as the town of Oberrittersgrün purchased the terminus station, track, a locomotive and a representative selection of rolling stock to establish a museum. The locomotive, Saxon Meyer No. 99 579, arrived under its own steam with the rolling stock in January 1972 – the very last train to run along the line. The station became the first railway museum in the GDR, and was, rather ironically, then taken over by Deutsche Reichsbahn, in 1984.

The line from Oschatz to Strehla closed in 1972, although the extension to the riverside quay had been abandoned earlier in 1957, and the track was removed shortly afterwards, largely using prison labour. However, that was not quite the end of the story, as in the 1980s most of the route was reused for a standard gauge railway, built entirely for strategic military reasons, to provide a link from Oschatz to Röderau, on the Elbe. Here, an alternative emergency bridge could be quickly put in place if required, providing a bypass to the main line river bridge via Riesa. The line was completed in 1987, but was never required for its intended purpose, being mainly used as a storage siding for redundant stock.

The network centred on Wilsdruff was gradually closed, with only the line between Freital Potschappel and Nossen remaining by 1972. A road replacement trial had been conducted on the Mohorn–Nossen section in May 1971, but that proved unacceptable, and the railway continued for the time being. In October 1972 the Mohorn–Freital line closed completely, with the Nossen end retained for freight. As the remaining locomotives could no longer be based at Wilsdruff, the facilities had to be reinstated at Nossen – a depot that had had overall responsibility for no less than seventy-six narrow gauge locomotives in 1945. It was a short reprieve, as soon only a short stub remained to serve a factory at Siebenlehn, and that went in December 1973, the end of the *Wilsdruffer Spinne*, or spider's web.

On 20 October 1971 a train en route from Klingenberg-Colmnitz to Frauenstein derailed near Oberbobritzsch and the locomotive overturned. The line was due to close at the end of the year anyway, but the accident resulted in the premature cessation of the service. The track on the line had deteriorated to such an extent, that the journey time on the 19-kilometre route was sixteen minutes longer than it had been pre-war.

A novel use was found for the line from Meinersdorf to Thum in 1974 when it was used to make a film based on the opera *Fra Diavolo*. For that reason, summer rail traffic was transferred to the roads, although passenger traffic ceased at the end of September in that year anyway. Two years earlier, the line from Thum to Wilischtal had closed, but a short length of around 1.6 kilometres was retained to serve a paper mill near Wilischtal. This traffic continued until 1992, operated by two small diesel locomotives, and it was only in 2005 that the track was dismantled.

In 1975, the government announced that four narrow gauge lines would, after all, be kept as passenger carrying tourist attractions and classed as technical monuments. The routes selected were:

Freital-Hainsberg–Kurort Kipsdorf
Radebeul Ost–Radeburg
Cranzahl–Oberwiesenthal
Zittau–Kurort Oybin and Kurort Jonsdorf

At this time several other lines were also still open, including the remaining section of the Mügeln network between Oschatz and Kemmlitz. This would lose its passenger traffic but be retained for the time being for the transport of kaolin from the mine at Kemmlitz. The other lines, from Wilkau Hasslau to Carlsfeld, and the Pressnitztalbahn from Wolkenstein to Jöhstadt would close. The Carlsfeld line succumbed in 1977, but remarkably the Jöhstadt line continued until 1986, and was the last line to close.

The various line closures had freed up surplus locomotives and rolling stock, and the better examples were distributed around those which would now remain. It was decided to refurbish and modernise the carriage stock, including the general fitting of steam heating, although the programme was only part completed at end of the GDR period. The trackwork, however, was in most cases in fairly poor condition, and although a programme of renewal was also announced, it too proceeded very slowly.

In 1981, the Soviet Union reduced oil supplies to the GDR, which forced the government to urgently review its transport policies. One result was a further longer-term reprieve for the freight only Kemmlitz traffic, and over the next two or three years the track was relaid from Oschatz. The conversion of this line to standard gauge was also seriously considered. The review did not, however, save the Pressnitztalbahn, which lost its passenger traffic in 1984, despite an upturn in traffic over the previous few years and finally closed to freight two years later. It was simply the poor condition of the track that led to the closure of the Steinbach–Jöhstadt section in 1984.

In 1971, an exhibition of historic rolling stock was held at Radebeul Ost station, featuring a variety of historic wagons, carriages and locomotives, some of which had been earmarked

The route between Kemmlitz and Oschatz survived with a freight service only. In 1980 a train approaches the Oschatz terminus. (Ed Kaas)

No. 1584 runs along a mixed gauge section of track at Oschatz with a train of empties for Kemmlitz in February 1980. (Ed Kaas)

No. 1574 approaches Mügeln in 1980. (Ed Kaas)

The cattle are clearly undisturbed by a double-headed working for Kemmlitz. (Ed Kaas)

Mügeln was the preserve of the Saxon Meyers, and four of the class rest on shed in the 1980s. (Ed Kaas)

for the Dresden Transport Museum. A number of early wagons and carriages had been set aside largely through the foresight of one or two individuals within the local railway management, and it was done at a time when the line was still threatened with closure within a few years. An enthusiast support group was established, which eventually became Traditionsbahn Radebeul, which since 1975 has run a series of special trains with historic stock on the Radebeul to Radeburg line. This was a groundbreaking concept in the GDR when first proposed and introduced.

By the late 1980s the railways were becoming evermore starved of investment, with more locomotives being withdrawn with serious defects, resulting in a proposal from Deutsche Reichsbahn to import diesel locomotives from Romania to replace the steam

A study of front ends at Mügeln. (Ed Kaas)

fleet. However, some track improvements were carried out on the Kurort Kipsdorf and Radeburg lines in an attempt to reduce journey times.

But then the Berlin wall fell, leading to a new political climate and whatever that might herald for the *bimmelbahnen*, or bell trains, the colloquial term for the narrow gauge railways, on account of the locomotive bells sounded near level crossings, and on sections of street running.

A passenger train enters Dippoldiswalde, bound for Freital-Hainsberg, surrounded by a healthy volume of freight traffic. (Ed Kaas)

No. 1761 crosses the viaduct approaching Malter station with a freight working in the mid-1980s. (Ed Kaas)

A variety of freight traffic was carried on the Weisseritztalbahn, including scrap metal from Schmiedeberg, as seen in this 1985 view. (A. Rickelt)

No. 1789 approaches Schmiedeberg with coal plus and an empty for the next load of scrap. (A. Rickelt)

A delightful view of a freight working crossing the Weisseritz river, in the Rabenau Gorge, 1989.
(Ed Kaas)

No. 1747 crosses
Schmiedeberg
Viaduct with
a freight train
consisting
of narrow
gauge wagons.
(Ed Kaas)

Above: No. 1777 crosse Scmiedeberg Viaduct with a passenger train in 1985. (A. Rickelt)

Below: On the Cranzahl to Oberwiesenthal line No. 1771 approaches Neudorf in February 1986. (Ed Kaas)

Above: A train from Radeburg, headed by No. 1788, runs alongside Pestalozzi Strasse as it approaches Radebeul Ost during the 1980s.

Below: A train headed by No. 1606 crosses the River Pressnitz, between Wolkenstein and Jöhstadt in December 1981. (Ed Kaas)

Above: No. 1606 shunts the yard at Wolkenstein. (Ed Kaas)

Below: The guard, wearing a Russian-style Reichsbahn hat, couples a *rollwagen* to the locomotive using an extension pole at Wolkenstein. (Ed Kaas)

Above: In this wintry scene No. 1606 runs alongside the River Prfessnitz with a mixed train for Jöhstadt. (Ed Kaas)

Below: The Pressnitztalbahn succombed to closure in 1986. Five years earlier No. 1606 ambles along the picturesque valley with a passenger train. (Ed Kaas)

4

Reunification and After

At German reunification in 1990 four passenger carrying railways were still operational, plus one freight-only line, all steam worked, and by 1992 it became clear that all would either be privatised or closed.

The line between Oschatz and Kemmlitz was in the most precarious position, as it relied on kaolin traffic from the mine at Kemmlitz, and it is worth noting that in the first year following reunification, rail freight traffic across the entire former East German Reichsbahn network halved. In November 1993, it passed from Deutsche Reichsbahn to a new company, Döllnitzbahn GmbH formed by the local authority and Berlin-based railway support group Pro

A train from Radebug to Radebeul passes a Trabant at a level crossing near Berbisdorf, not long after the collapse of the DDR in September 1990. (Neil Knowlden)

Above: Freight was still carried on the Radeburg line in 1990, and in this chaotic scene a standard gauge hopper has fallen from its transporter wagon. (Neil Knowlden)

Below: The breakdown gang prepare to jack up another standard gauge wagon. (Neil Knowlden)

Above: No. 1771, one of the 1950s-built locomotives, heads a train southwards across Malter Viaduct bound for Kurort Kipsdorf on 17 September 1990. (Neil Knowlden)

Below: On a wet day in April 1991, a train passes through Freital-Cossmannsdorf bound for Freital-Hainsberg. (Neil Knowlden)

Above: In 1990 Class IV K locomotive No. 1606 was retained for occasional use with engineering trains... (A. Rickelt)

Below: ...which could entail an impromptu stop for water en route. (A. Rickelt)

Above: A train from Cranzahl to Oberwiesenthal headed by No. 1776 blasts its way alongside the Czech border near Unterwiesenthal in May 1991. (Neil Knowlden)

Below: No. 1758 waits at Zittau for its 12.10 departure to Kurort Jonsdorf on 28 April 1991. (Neil Knowlden)

Above: At the end of the branch to Kurort Oybin No. 1750 runs around its train. (Neil Knowlden)

Below: No. 1758 approaches Kurort Jonsdorf with its train in April 1991. (Neil Knowlden)

No. 1757 trundles across a steel viaduct at Olbersdorf, near the border territory south of Zittau. (Neil Knowlden)

Bahn with the aim of keeping the kaolin traffic. The line was still worked entirely by Meyer IV K locomotives, with freight carried exclusively in standard gauge wagons for transfer to the main line. However, the new owners acquired two diesel locomotives from Poland, and some narrow gauge wagons from the eastern Harz region, and built a new transhipment facility at Oschatz. Despite initial optimism, the traffic level gradually declined and ceased completely in 2001 – the last narrow gauge line in Saxony to carry freight. Remarkably, the new owners managed to reinstate a school contract passenger service between Altmügeln and Oschatz in 1995, which for a period around the turn of the millennium reverted to steam operation because the newly acquired diesels were unserviceable.

A supporting enthusiast group using the name Wilder Robert – which had long been the colloquial name for the railway – was also formed with the aim of developing steam-hauled tourist traffic and the organisation of special events.

In 2006, the line from Nebitzschen to Glossen reopened, where it linked with the local Feldbahn museum, which has preserved part of a 600-mm quarry railway, including the loading facility at Glossen. In the same year the state garden show was held at Oschatz, which provided a major boost for the railway.

However, there were setbacks, and in 2011 the railway was faced with the imminent withdrawal of financial support, necessitating appeals to other authorities, which secured funding for a further two years. In 2013, the railway became closely integrated with the company now operating the Zittau lines, and a further seven years of financial support was granted, with the line being integrated into the Leipzig regional transport area. Unlike the other lines which survived, the Oschatz – Mügeln route is not in an area with substantial tourism, and is more heavily reliant on subsidised local traffic.

Deutsche Bahn, the operator of the reunited Germany's rail network, did not really want to keep any of the steam narrow gauge lines that it found itself responsible for in 1994, and threatened closure if they could not be sold off to private concerns. An early interim action was to transfer them to a subsidiary company.

The operation of the lines at Zittau was transferred to a new private company, Sächsische Oberlausitzer Eisenbahngesellschaft, (SOEG), a subsidiary of the regional bus operator, in December 1996, which embarked on an extensive programme of permanent way upgrading and other infrastructure improvements. Other commercial and marketing innovations included the introduction of a bar/buffet car and two carriages with wheelchair access. In 2005, the railway carried 95,000 passengers, and the company became detached from the bus operator, and as mentioned above, has become very closely associated with the Döllnitzbahn. Prior to privatisation in 1993, the locomotives based at Zittau were converted to oil firing, with carriages being converted from vacuum to air brakes as standard. The railway has since reverted to coal firing. Both the Zittau and Oschatz lines have diesel locomotives from Romania, and the Oschatz line also has a more modern diesel railcar, completely refurbished and upgraded in 2015.

Again, a support group had been formed which, even before privatisation, established a museum in the goods shed at Kurort Oybin station, and which has more recently also taken over Bertsdorf station building.

The fate of the line from Cranzahl to Oberwiesenthal attracted the attention of the regional authority in Annaberg Buchholz, which recognised its importance and potential in developing all-year-round tourist traffic in the area. Thus, it was the next line to be transferred to a new operator, BVO Bahn, again, a subsidiary of the regional bus operator, which took over from 4 May 1998. This concern later became the Sächsische Dampfeisenbahn Gesellschaft, or Saxon Steam Railway Company. There was even a proposal to extend the line from Cranzahl to Annaberg Buccholz – this was a period when the standard gauge line remained closed for an extended period awaiting reconstruction, but eventually this idea was abandoned. Oberwiesenthal is the highest town in eastern Germany, adjoining the Czech border, with winter sports facilities, and the new operator lost no time in promoting the potential source of traffic, also introducing the brand name Fichtelbergbahn – taking its name from the Fichtel mountain near Oberwiesenthal. In 2004, a new locomotive shed and workshop was opened at Oberwiesenthal, and the new regime has invested in track renewal and the reconstruction of the Hüttenbach Viaduct.

This transfer left DB with the two lines close to Dresden. While the line from Radebeul Ost carried tourist traffic to Moriztburg, for visitors to the castle, the further section to Radeburg attracted considerably less traffic. The other route, from Freital-Hainsberg to Kurort Kipsdorf is a delightfully scenic route, but like its neighbour, hopelessly uneconomic. Both lines operated a two-train service to maintain a basic two-hourly interval throughout the day, which entailed lengthy unremunerative layovers at each end. Goods traffic survived on the Freital-Hainsberg line until 1994, serving a scrap yard at Schmiedeberg, and two coal merchants en route.

The regional transport authority gave DB a fifteen-year financial subsidy in 1998, which allowed for some much needed investment.

Trackwork needed heavy expenditure and the Radebeul line was closed for a period of several months for permanent way work. However, much of the work was defective, resulting in a further period of closure for remedial work.

Then in summer 2002 disaster struck the Kurort Kipsdorf route. That August heavy rainfall caused severe flooding, and the River Elbe rose some eight metres above normal levels. The city of Dresden was badly hit, and on 12 August a torrent of water in the Weisseritz Valley destroyed large sections of the narrow gauge line, particularly through the scenic Rabenau Gorge. A complete train was stranded at Dippoldiswalde, the midway station, and the town itself was virtually cut off with roads also destroyed. The locomotive and carriages were removed by road somewhile later. The damage was so severe that few imagined that the line would ever be rebuilt, although in December 2002 a few special trains were run over the relatively unscathed section between Dippoldiswalde and Seifersdorf.

In 2004, BVO Bahn took over both the Radebeul and Freital lines, branding the former Lössnitzgrundbahn and the latter Weisseritztalbahn – which at this point was not an operable railway. Work started on planning the reconstruction of the line, although it would be another three years before funding was procured and contracts were signed for the first stage, the rebuilding of the line from Freital to Dippoldiswalde. Regular services recommenced on this section on 14 December 2008. Meanwhile, in 2007, BVO Bahn, by now renamed SDG Sächsische Dampfeisenbahn Gesellschaft, sold a 35 per cent holding in the company to the regional transport authority, Zweckverband Verkehrsverbund Oberelbe (ZVOE).

In November 2012, a train operated for a few days on an isolated upper section of the line between Obercarsdorf and Schmiedeberg, but it was to be August 2014 before the first

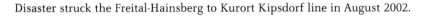

Disaster struck the Freital-Hainsberg to Kurort Kipsdorf line in August 2002.

Above: Severe flooding destroyed most of the line through the scenic Rabenau Gorge.

Below: It was to be six years before the lower part of the line was rebuilt, but No. 1746 is seen here after arrival at Dippoldiswalde, the temporary terminus, a few days after reopening in December 2008.

Fortunately, the entire line eventually reopened, and a train prepares for departure from Freital-Hainsberg for Kipsdorf in August 2018.

contract to rebuild four bridges on the upper section was let. This was followed by a further contract to reinstate the remainder of the line, which was let in March 2016. Nearly fifteen years after the disastrous floods, the line reopened throughout on 17 June 2017. Since the reopening the line has operated a one-train timetable, with only two journeys daily over the full length of the line, plus a short working between Freital and Dippoldiswalde. An innovative feature of the rebuilt railway is the use of recycled plastic sleepers between Dippoldiswalde and Kurort Kipsdorf.

Likewise, the operation at Radebeul has been cut back to a one-train timetable, with two daily round trips to Radeburg and several intermediate workings to Moritzburg. Remarkably, there is still also an additional schooldays-only service, which leaves Radebeul Ost at 05.15, returning from Radeburg at 06.25 – even as late as 2020 a steam-hauled narrow gauge school train appeared in the suburbs of a major city in Germany. An announcement in 2011 had indicated that financial pressures might force the closure of the Moritzburg to Radeburg section, or perhaps use cheaper railcar operation.

The privately run railways are keen to hold special events and run special trains, sometimes with the help of local support groups, with such activities on the Lossnitzgrundahn dating back to the 1970s.

Unfortunately, it was during a gala weekend, celebrating the 125th anniversary of the line in 2009, that two trains were involved in a serious collision near Friedewald station. Over 100 passengers were injured, and one of the locomotives involved was visiting from the Mansfelder Bergwerksbahn, a museum railway in the eastern Harz region. Even more unfortunately, it was the second accident that day, as earlier a train double-headed by two IV K locomotives had hit a car on a level crossing.

Apart from the survival of the lines that were still in regular operation, several enthusiast-led heritage railways and static museums have been established. The Pressnitztalbahn, which ran between Wolkenstein and Jöhstadt, had only closed as recently as 1986, and demolition work was still underway when the first ideas of a museum railway were mooted in 1989. In the following year, with the change in political climate, a formal group was established with the aim of reopening a section of the railway as a working museum. One of the first achievements was the restoration of the locomotive shed at the terminus station Jöhstadt, although unfortunately most of the original station site was lost for redevelopment. Over the following years the line was gradually rebuilt as far as Steinbach, and the railway successfully achieved EU funding for a new carriage shed at Jöhstadt. While the museum railway is largely volunteer run, operating mainly weekends only, in 2008 the organisation took over a commercially operated narrow gauge steam railway, with year-round daily service, plus the franchise for the connecting standard gauge branch line, on the island of Rügen. Another company was set up in order to do this, the Eisenbahn-Bau- und Betriebsgesellschaft Pressnitztalbahn, and it is indeed a very different type of operation from the original museum line.

In 2006 a new organisation, the VSSB, founded to promote the Saxon narrow gauge lines, made a decision to construct a new replica I K 0-6-0T locomotive. Archive drawings were discovered, and after an intense fundraising campaign the locomotive was built at the steam locomotive works at Meiningen. The locomotive was completed just three years later in June 2009, with a formal launch by the Prime Minister of Saxony, Stanislaw Tillich

The Zittau system has continued to prosper, and No. 749 is seen heading south in summer 2017. (Steve Dymott)

Above: Continued investment in the privatised railways has included new workshop facilities at Oberwiesenthal. (Steve Dymott)

Below: Class VI K No. 715 waits to depart from Jöhstadt, with a Pressnitztalbahn Christmas service in December 2008.

Above: The Jöhstadt-based museum railway attracted EU funding for a substantial new carriage shed facility. (Steve Dymott)

Below: Preserved at Bertsdorf is No. 99 4532, a locomotive originally built for the Trusetalbahn in Thüringen, but for many years used as a shunter at Zittau. (Steve Dymott)

at Radebeul. The engine was then based at Jöhstadt until 2015, but has since been based at Zittau, although regular visits are made to other railways for special events.

Further west, at Schönheide, another scheme was initiated in 1991 to preserve part of the line which ran from Wilkau Hasslau to Carlsfeld. The locomotive shed at Schönheide Mitte was restored and work started to reinstate the 4-kilometre length of line to Stützengrün, which had been the last section of the whole line to close in 1977. It had been retained to serve a brush factory adjacent to the station at Stützengrün. The original intention was to rebuild the line to its former southern terminus at Carlsfeld, as the earlier demolition of the viaduct beyond Stützengrün would prevent further expansion northwards. In its early days the museum acquired a diesel locomotive from Wilischtal paper mill, two IV K steam locomotives, plus an assortment of carriages and wagons. The first of the Meyers was restored over the next two years and was in steam again in 1994 and operated as far as Neuheide.

In 1998, the museum abandoned its proposal to extend the line to Carlsfeld, but the following year another group, the Förderverein Historische Westsächsische Eisenbahnen was formed with the idea of reopening not only that section of line, but the former standard gauge line from Schönheide Ost to Muldenburg. Track was relaid at both Carlsberg and Schönheide Süd stations, and then in 2009 an even more ambitious scheme was announced, which involved the construction of a brand-new narrow gauge line to Wernesgrün, with a total price tag approaching €20 million. The project was designed to further develop tourism in the Vogtland/western Erzgebirge region, and although initially supported by the various local and regional authorities, the costs were too great and the overall scheme abandoned. However, undeterred, the FHWE is still intent on reopening the standard gauge line, with the recreation of the narrow gauge project further into the future. One major obstacle to overcome will be a missing bridge near Schönheide Süd.

The original museum line has since concentrated its efforts on its own 4-kilometre line, operating on about twelve weekends each year, with its two Meyer IV K steam engines and authentic heritage stock.

Smaller-scale museum sites have been set up, representing other closed lines. The old locomotive shed at Wilsdruff, once an important narrow gauge junction, has been purchased by the community and converted into a museum. Although the last trains had long since departed and the track lifted shortly thereafter, the building was retained for servicing diesel engines, only finally closing in 1996. A short length of track has been relaid, offering draisine rides, while the museum itself, open on selected weekends each year, exhibits various full-size items of stock and models of the old station area.

The Schwarzbachbahn, which operated between Gossdorf Kohlmühle and Hohnstein in 'Saxon Switzerland', was closed as long ago as 1951 and the track lifted almost immediately, but fortunately most of the route and structure survived. In 1995, a local group was set up with the long-term aim of rebuilding the entire line, initialling establishing a base and laying track at Lohsdorf station. There were also hopes of acquiring a IV K locomotive, No. 99 555, which had been statically preserved for some years at Gera, but this was ultimately unsuccessful, and it went to Zittau. However, a steam engine was returned to Lohsdorf for an inaugural event in 2005, and other festivals, with visiting engines operating over the museum's short length of track have been held at intervals since. However, plans to revive the particularly scenic route to Gossdorf Kohlmühle suffered a major setback in late 2019, when the scheme was rejected by the National Park authority on environmental grounds, although a few months later plans were still being finalised to rebuild further concrete bridges en route.

The main commercial railways now seem to be secure for the foreseeable future, although several are very heavily reliant on financial support. All have benefitted from major track renewals in recent years, and other infrastructure improvements – large sections of the Weisseritztalbahn are in effect new railway as a result of the 2002 floods. Zittau and Oberwiesenthal have invested in new locomotive facilities, and at the former, carriage facilities too. Whereas in the days of a single operator locomotives and carriages would be sent away to Nossen or Görlitz for repair and overhaul, the individual railway operators are now responsible for their own stock. Apart from the regular steam services, all have embraced heritage operation and special events too. The Döllnitzbahn offers regular weekend steam services with its IV K locomotives, and the Zittau system is now home to its own IV K, No. 99 555, the new-build I K, with a complete Saxon railways vintage train, and the restored railcar VT 137 322. Vintage trains continue to operate on occasional weekends on the Lössnitzgrundbahn under the auspices of Traditionsbahn Radebeul, as they have done since the mid-1970s. Zittau is also the home of another interesting locomotive, an 0-8-0T, which carries the number 99 4532, and was originally built in 1924 for the Trusebahn, which ran between Trusetal and Wernshausen in the neighbouring state of Thuringia. Displaced by larger engines it came to Zittau in 1963 and worked as a shunting locomotive until the boiler was condemned in 1989. It is now preserved in the engine shed at Bertsdorf.

The narrow gauge railways are recognised as an important and integral part of the region's tourist industry, and a joint marketing campaign promotes the 'steam route Saxony'.

New-build Saxon I K locomotive No. 54 with heritage stock at Lohsdorf, base of the Schwarzbach museum railway project. (Schwarzbachbahn collection)

5

Locomotives and Rolling Stock

The first trains in October 1881 on the newly opened line between Wilkau and Kirchberg were worked by a contractor's locomotive, but just one month later Saxon State Railways introduced the first of a class of six coupled-tank locomotives, which would become known as their l K class from 1900, and eventually totalling thirty-nine in number. They were built by Richard Hartmann (Sächsische Maschinefabrik) at Chemnitz, which also built a further five engines in 1890 for the Zittau lines, which at that time were operated by a private company. The four Zittau engines were numbered 1–4 and were actually named: *Mandau, Lausche, Töpfer*, and *Hochwald*. A fifth engine named *Zittau* followed a year later.

A works view of Saxon I K class 0-6-0T, No. 41, with the Heberlein brake cabling clearly evident.

New-build replica Class I K No. 54 at Oschatz in 2010.

Five engines were left in Poland after the First World War, but twenty-seven were still working at the Reichsbahn takeover, although all were then withdrawn within a few years. One locomotive, sold for further industrial use, remained at work in Schmiedeberg ironworks for a further forty years.

It was not long before the railways were looking for more powerful locomotives, yet able to negotiate some fairly tortuous curves, and in 1885 two double-ended Fairlie types were ordered from Hawthorn Leslie, in Newcastle, England. They were designated HthFTK, but later class II K, and numbered 18 and 19. They were unpopular with footplate crews from the outset, and to add to their woes were too heavy for many routes, with the result that one was withdrawn in 1903 and the other six years later.

In 1913, four I K class engines were taken into works and adapted to run as two pairs, with the rear of each cab removed and coupled back to back, with integrated controls. As such they were also designated Class II K. The outbreak of war disrupted proposals for further conversions, partly because of demands from the army for locomotives, and in 1916 the four previously adapted reverted to their original form.

In 1889, two 0-6-2T locomotives were ordered from Krauss, which used the Klose system of articulation, whereby leading and trailing driven axles were able to move radially to negotiate curves, and the trailing wheels were also articulated which necessitated a jointed bunker and cab roof. The design was made even more complex by the use of inside cylinders with outside valves, and valve gear by Klose, who was at this time chief engineer of the

One of a pair of double-ended Fairlie-type locomotives built in the UK by Hawthorn Leslie in 1885.

A pair of I K locomotives converted to operate as a double-ended entity in 1913. The locomotives reverted to original form three years later.

Württemberg State Railways. Four more examples were built by Hartmann, and although good performers they suffered from high maintenance costs, and were withdrawn by 1927. Latterly, two were based on the Müglitztalbahn working between Heidenau and Altenburg, but the class had long been employed on the Wolkenstein to Jöhstadt and also Cranzahl

The Class III K 0-6-2T locomotives were introduced in 1889.

Class III K No. 36 is seen here at Oberrittersgrün c. 1900. (Oberrittersgrün Railway Museum)

to Oberwiesenthal routes. Initially classed as K KI T K, they became Class III K. The prototype of the design had been built in 1885 for Bosnia, which eventually took delivery of thirty-four locomotives, some of which could still be found working in the mid-1960s.

However, there were advantages in using articulated locomotives, and in 1892 Saxon State Railways introduced a new design, which in time would become the most numerous class with ninety-six examples built. The design was based on the Günther Meyer principle, with two four-wheel articulated bogies, one driven with high and the other with low pressure cylinders, thus an 0-4-4-0T arrangement, and a conventional locomotive boiler. The articulation allowed these fairly lengthy engines to cope with the most severe curves, and therefore offer maximum route availability.

The locomotives were built by Richard Hartmann at Chemnitz over a thirty-year period from 1892 until 1921. Originally the class designation was HMTKV, which could be analysed as:

H – Built by Hartmann
M – Designed using Meyer principle
T – Tank locomotive, confusingly, however, the German term is *tenderlok*
K – Narrow gauge, i.e. Kleinspur
V – Compound locomotive, i.e. Verbund

Later they would be reclassified as the IV K Class, by which they are well known today.

They were an immediate success and could be found across the entire network with both freight and passenger traffic. Following the First World War three engines were

The most numerous locomotive type was the Meyer IV K Class, epitomised by No. 1568, simmering in Oschatz Yard in April 1991. (Neil Knowlden)

The different sizes of high- and low-pressure cylinders can be seen in this view of a IV K loaded within a standard gauge freight train at Annaberg-Buchholz in 1991. (Neil Knowlden)

A Meyer bogie under overhaul at Mareinburg Works in early 2020. (Andre Dorfelt)

passed to Poland as reparations, while a further two never returned from wartime duties in Hungary. Although there were some withdrawals in the 1930s, and nine engines were sent to railways elsewhere in Germany, there were still nearly sixty on the books after the Second World War.

The Saxon V K Class were eight-coupled locomotives built especially for the steeply graded Müglitztalbahn, with a total of nine built between 1901 and 1907. With outside frames, they were fitted with Klein-Lindner axles to allow greater flexibility on the tight curves, a method invented by two engineers employed by Saxon State Railways. They were also compound locomotives with a 340-mm-diameter high-pressure cylinder and 530-mm-diameter low-pressure cylinder. Like the III K Class they proved expensive to maintain, but remained on the Altenburg line until it was converted to standard gauge. Thereafter they were transferred to other lines, although it is believed that all were withdrawn by 1942.

In the early days trains were braked by means of the Heberlein system, whereby brakes on each vehicle are applied by means of a continuous cable running the length of the train at carriage roof level. Should a cable snap it is a failsafe system, and, although largely superseded in general use by the vacuum brake in the 1920s, it was still in limited use until as late as 1987 and can still be seen on some heritage lines today. In the late 1980s and early 1990s the remaining lines were converted from vacuum to air brakes.

The first ten-coupled locomotives on the Saxon narrow gauge were a batch of fifteen built in 1918 by Henschel to an order for military use in Poland. The end of hostilities meant that they were not used for their original purpose, but were sold to the Saxon State Railways and designated Class VI K. A further forty-seven were built between 1923 and 1927 after the Reichsbahn takeover, although not all were for use in Saxony. Several of the earlier engines were sent to Austria, and three were taken by the Soviet Union in 1945. In the 1960s seven engines were completely rebuilt at Görlitz, and the result was in effect a

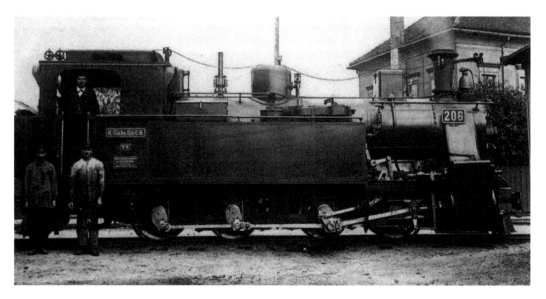

The eight-coupled Saxon V K Class was designed specifically for the Müglitztalbahn.

A detail of the Heberlein cable-operated braking mechanism.

The cable extends at roof level along the length of the train.

A detail of the Scharfenberg coupling, with steam heat and air brake hoses. (Steve Dymott)

batch of more or less new engines with replacement frames, welded boilers, cylinders and much else. The class had been fitted with superheated boilers from new, and originally the fourth coupled axle took the drive, with the first, third and fifth axles allowed lateral movement using the Gölsdorf principle. On the rebuilt engines, the second and fourth axles had the lateral movement, while the third axle now took the drive.

All the remaining VI Ks were withdrawn in 1975, and although four are preserved only two are based in Saxony: No. 99 713 at Radebeul and No. 99 715 at Jöhstadt.

Soon after the formation of Deutsche Reichsbahn it embarked upon a programme of standard locomotive designs, referred to as Einheitslokomotiven, and production for the system, including the narrow gauge lines. The design for the 750-mm gauge lines, which became known as the 99.73-76 Class, was a development of the existing powerful ten-coupled locomotives, but with the addition of leading and trailing pony trucks, plus bar frames. As originally built the centre driving axle had narrower flanges than the other coupled wheels, but these were later removed completely to allow tighter curves to be negotiated. The boilers were fitted with feedwater heaters, located on top of the smokebox, and although the locomotives were fitted with an air brake, it was designed to work with a vacuum-braked train, and the Heberlein cable system, which was still in regular use.

The first batch of thirteen locomotives was built by Sächsische Maschinenfabrik, the company name for Richard Hartmann, in 1928, and were an immediate success. The Chemnitz builder collapsed soon after, and subsequent orders were completed by Berliner Maschinebau, bringing the class total to thirty-two.

One of the surviving members of the VI K Class. No .713 is pictured at Freital-Hainsberg in July 2018. (C. Gebhart)

The impressive Einheitslokomotiven were first introduced in 1928. No. 1741 is seen in the shed at Freital-Hainsberg. (Steve Dymott)

Deutsche Reichsbahn also set about establishing a standardised system of numbering for its steam locomotives soon after its formation. All narrow gauge engines were grouped within series prefixed 99, followed by the locomotives own number. In July 1970, DR introduced a more complex scheme, retaining the prefix 99, with a four-digit locomotive serial number and a seventh 'check' digit, separated by a dash. For 750-mm gauge steam locomotives the first digit of the serial number was normally 1 to indicate coal firing, and the 'check' digit was the result of applying a mathematical formula to the other digits. Today, examples of both earlier and later numbering schemes can be seen on many of the railways in Saxony.

The Soviet Union took ten Einheits engines as war reparations in 1945, and this action, coupled with a backlog of maintenance, resulted in a severe shortage of serviceable locomotives.

To address this, the design was slightly modified as Class 99.77-79, and twenty-four locomotives were ordered from the Karl Marx works at Babelsberg in Berlin and delivered between 1952 and 1957. The Karl Marx works had been part of the firm Orenstein & Koppel, which had found itself under the communist regime, and it was only with some difficulty that the Reichsbahn was able to place the order, as the works were also heavily engaged in building new locomotives for the Soviet Union. Initially the new engines were allocated to Freital-Hainsberg, which took the first one in August 1952, Cranzahl, Thum and Wilsdruff. Known as Neubau, or new-build, locomotives, they had larger fireboxes than the earlier engines, and also welded plate frames rather than bar construction.

No. 1789, seen here being coaled at Radebeul, represents the Neubau locomotives built in the 1950s. (Steve Dymott)

At the same time the Karl Marx works was also engaged in building a class of narrow gauge 0-8-0 tender locomotives as war reparations for the Soviet Union. They were wood fired and intended for use on forestry railways, but the prototype of the class, which totalled over 400 locomotives, was trialled on the Weisseritztalbahn between Freital-Hainsberg and Kurort Kipsdorf over several weeks in September and October 1954.

Despite the introduction of the Neubau locomotives in the 1950s, and subsequent plans for replacement diesels, there was still a shortage of serviceable motive power. Government financial constraints prevented further new builds, thus in 1962 DR embarked on a programme of extensive rebuilds of the Saxon Meyer IV K Class. The locomotives that emerged from works were in many respects new engines, like the seven rebuilt VI K locomotives mentioned above, with new welded boilers, and most had new frames and cylinders too, frequently with new cabs and tanks as well. They could be visually distinguished from their un-rebuilt counterparts by their flat-topped domes. Three of the last of the original locomotives were retained for preservation when they were withdrawn in the 1970s, but remarkably there were still thirteen operational at the formation of the integrated Deutsche Bahn in 1991. In particular, the Oschatz–Mügeln–Kemmlitz line was completely Meyer-worked. Over twenty of the class have survived into the preservation era. Several have remained in more or less continuous service, while others have been acquired by heritage railways and returned to steam. Further examples reside in museums, with one, No. 99 534, statically preserved with a carriage at Geyer, in the community it once served, while No. 99 535 can be seen in the Dresden Transport Museum.

During the 1980s a number of Neubau 2-10-2T locomotives were withdrawn with unserviceable boilers and serious frame defects, and a few years later in 1991 new frames and boilers were constructed at Meiningen works for a total of fourteen engines, with the locomotives being reassembled at Görlitz. The works at Görlitz had had a long history of overhauling narrow gauge locomotives, but with the forthcoming change in structure of the entire railway network, this was phased out, and the works finally closed in 1997. However, the locomotive works at Meiningen, in the neighbouring state of Thuringia, was retained by the new united Deutsche Bahn, and still regularly overhauls steam engines from the various narrow gauge concerns.

In the 1980s stock was gradually converted from vacuum to air braking, but there was still occasional use of the Heberlein cable brakes until as late as 1987. One of the earliest sections to be converted to air brake was the line between Lommatzsch and Nossen, as a result of two accidents at Gorsbach caused by cable brakes becoming caked in ice. The first in 1949 had left four dead, and the second also caused one fatality on Christmas Day 1962.

In 1938, DR ordered four prototype diesel railcars for the narrow gauge system from Waggon und Maschinefabrik vorm Busch, based in Bautzen. Originally fitted with a Vomag eight-cylinder horizontal engine with hydraulic transmission, two had a nominal seating capacity of thirty-four while the other two had luggage compartment and reduced seating and were numbered VT 137 322–5. They were used on the lines at Zittau, and despite some teething problems, they proved successful, usually operating in two-car sets. However, although they were much more economical in operation than steam-hauled trains, they were laid up at the outbreak of war in 1939 in order to conserve fuel oil. In 1943, they were requisitioned, and although three were sent to Poznan, in Poland, VT 137 322 was damaged during the loading process and left behind. After the war it was repaired and reinstated, remaining in service until 1964, thereafter languishing in the engine shed at Bertsdorf for many years. Although acquired by the Dresden Transport Museum in 1980, it remained in store until restoration by the railway's new operator in 1995.

Towards the end of the war in 1944 three railcar sets that had been built for the Latvian state railway arrived in Germany with its retreating army. Although several cars were then subsequently badly damaged in an air raid, a three-car unit was rebuilt from them all, consisting of two passenger cars with a central, shorter, power car with two Mercedes engines. This was put to work in 1951 running between Freital Potschappel and Nossen, but three years later it was sent to Zittau, and finally in 1957 it was sent to the Baltic island of Rügen.

In 1960, two prototype diesel locomotives, were built by the Karl Marx works at Babelsberg, and numbered V 36 4801 and 4802. They were initially sent to Wilsdruff for trials, and it was hoped to build a further batch of twelve, as replacements for steam locomotives. Although they were a powerful design, they suffered from a variety of teething issues, but the major problem preventing their more general use was their heavy axle loading at over 10 tons. They were tried on other routes, but after two years they were stored at Bertsdorf and finally scrapped.

VT 137 322 is the sole survivor of the four diesel railcars built in 1938, seen here at Kurort Oybin in 2017. (Steve Dymott)

In 1989, Deutsche Reichsbahn announced that diesel locomotives would be imported from Romania to largely replace the steam fleet, but that was shortly before the collapse of the government, and a dramatic change in the political landscape.

Most lines now have at least one small diesel for shunting, but the Döllnitzbahn has its two larger former Romanian diesels, plus a railcar and trailer from Austria, which were acquired in 2017. The 1995-built railcar was refurbished and modernised at the Jenbach works of the Zillertalbahn before transfer to Germany. The trailer had formerly operated on the Mariazellerbahn.

The first carriages were wooden-bodied four-wheelers, but by the turn of the century new bogie carriages with clerestory roofs, a loading balcony and doors at each end were becoming more common. In the 1920s the railways were losing traffic to newly introduced competing bus services, and the recently formed Deutsche Reichsbahn responded with the introduction of more new 'standard' bogie passenger coaches in 1928, with vacuum train brakes superseding the old Heberlein system, and steam heating. Trains were now normally single class. Scharfenberg semi-automatic couplings were now also adopted as standard, replacing the earlier 'funnel' couplings, which had the disadvantage of 'male' and 'female' ends. In 1933, five older clerestory roofed coaches were converted into open-top 'cabrio' passenger cars, two of which survive, but further coaches have been similarly converted in more recent years. Although many lines ceased to carry mail in the post-war years, two new narrow gauge vans were built for Deutsche Post.

The programme of closures in the 1960s led to the withdrawal of many coaches and wagons, but regardless of their condition all were outmoded as a regular means of transport. In 1974 DR embarked on a modernisation programme, to upgrade sufficient stock for the

Above: Two Romanian-built diesel locomotives rest in the Döllnitzbahn's shed at Mügeln. (Steve Dymott)

Below: Even with daily steam operation, all lines have a small diesel available for shunting, such as this example built by LKM at Babelsberg. (Steve Dynott)

Above: The 1995-built railcar acquired from the Austrian Zillertalbahn for use on the Döllnitzbahn, is seen here at Kurort Oybin in 2017. (Steve Dymott)

Below: A third-class, four-wheel carriage in Saxon Sate Railways livery, preserved at Radebeul Ost. (Steve Dymott)

Clerestory-roofed bogie carriage preserved at Rittersgrün museum station. (Steve Dymott)

remaining lines. The work was carried out at Perleberg Works, Wittenberg. Each carriage body was dismantled to a skeleton framework, and then fitted with new prefabricated steel side panels, roof structure, thermal insulation, flooring and aluminium-framed side windows – the latter of the same pattern as those fitted to the standard gauge double-deck stock at that time. Steel seat frames, upholstered with synthetic leather, replaced the old wooden slatted variety, and the refurbishment included new electric lighting, sliding end doors, and steam heating. New toilets were fitted, although still without the luxury of water! The modernisation programme included all the narrow gauge lines in East Germany which were to be retained, and the first refurbished Saxon carriage went to the Cranzahl–Oberwiesenthal line in 1977, with three more passenger cars plus a luggage van for Freital-Hainsberg the following year.

In 1982, it was established that a new standardised structure could be fitted to all 750-mm and 1,000-mm-gauge carriages (of which the Harz network operated a large number), allowing further economy of scale in the rebuilding programme. In the following year new wheelsets with roller bearings were fitted for the first time.

In the early years of the Saxon narrow gauge, second- and third-class travel was offered, with the addition of fourth class from 1913. By the mid-1960s the Radebeul–Radeburg route was the only one still offering passengers a choice of first- and second-class travel. All were second class only at the end of the GDR era. The first carriages had no heating, but were later fitted with stoves, which could be removed during the summer months – steam heating was only introduced with the new 1920s standard stock and locomotives. Despite

Above: An example of a rebuilt carriage with moderised windows, yet retaining earlier style balcony roof at Radebeul. (Steve Dymott)

Below: Many carriages still in use today were completely rebuilt with new framework and roof profiles. (Steve Dymott)

the introduction of electric lighting at the same time, some gas-lit carriages remained in use until as late as 1975.

Although many carriages were refurbished and modernised, a large number of un-rebuilt examples still survived when the Perleberg works closed in 1992 – some still with stoves for heating!

More recently BVO Bahn, which initially took over the Cranzahl, Radeburg and Freital-Hainsberg lines established a carriage overhaul and repair facility at Marienberg, alongside its commercial vehicle workshop. By 2020 the company, now renamed Regionalverkehr Erzgebirge (RVE), was additionally able to offer steam locomotive services, for example frame repairs and platework fabrication. While in DR days narrow gauge locomotives and stock would normally be transported to and from works by the main line railways, today all such movements are made by road transport.

The private operators have continued to invest in their carriage stock, and adapt to modern requirements, with the introduction of wheelchair accessible features, more open 'cabrio' passenger cars, and refreshment bar cars in some trains.

The first wagons were four-wheel vehicles, but bogie types were constructed from the turn of the century onwards. Apart from open wagons and box vans, some bolster wagons were built for the transport of logs and other lengthy items. As discussed previously, it was not long before the facility to transport standard gauge wagons was introduced, using either *rollbock* bogies or transporter wagons, which were built with a variety of different lengths. Special loading facilities, usually either a ramp and/or pit were needed to position and secure the full-sized wagons.

Interior view of heritage stock at Zittau, which demonstrates the amount of space occupied by the heating stoves. (Steve Dymott)

Above: A general view of SDG's locomotive workshop at Marienberg, with 2-10-2 and Meyer locomotives undergoing overhaul in April 2020. (Andre Dorfelt)

Below: Most of the commercial operators regularly include 'cabrio' open carriages in train formations during the summer months. (Steve Dymott)

Above: A carriage modernised and adapted with a wheelchair lift for the Zittau system. (Steve Dymott)

Below: A snowplough in summer storage at Radebeul Ost, 2015. (Steve Dymott)

Locomotive Summary. 750-mm-gauge Saxon State Lines

Type	Saxon State Numbers	DR Numbers	Builder	Date Built	
I K	1–4, 6–17, 20–34, 37–42, 47–53 ZOJE 1–5 *	99 7501–7527	Sächsische Maschinefabrik, Chemnitz	1881–1892	
II K (Original)	18, 19	N/A	Hawthorn Leslie, Newcastle UK	1885	
II K (I K rebuild)	61 A/B	99 7551	Sächsische Maschinefabrik Chemnitz	Rebuilt 1913 from locos 1 and 4	
	62 A/B	N/A	Sächsische Maschinefabrik Chemnitz	Rebuilt 1913 from locos 2 and 3	
III K	35, 36	99 7541/2	Krauss	1889	
	43–46	99 7543–6	Sächsische Maschinefabrik, Chemnitz	1891	
IV K	103–198	99 511–608	Sächsische Maschinefabrik, Chemnitz	1892–1921	
V K	201–209	99 611–619	Sächsische Maschinefabrik, Chemnitz	1901–1907	
VI K	210–224	99 641–655	Henschel	1918–19	
	N/A	99 671– 717	Henschel, Sächsische Maschinefabrik Maschinebau Karlsruhe	1923–27	
99. 73 - 76	N/A	99 731–762	Sächsische Maschinefabrik, Berliner Maschinebau	1928–33	
99.77 - 79	N/A	99 771–794	Karl Marx Lokomotivebau, Babelsberg	1952–56	

Note: The firm Sächsische Maschinefabrik is also often referred to by the name of its founder, Richard Hartmann. The company name was introduced in 1870, but following a restructuring in 1898 it became Sächsische Maschinefabrik vormals Richard Hartmann AG.

Dates Withdrawn	Wheel Arrangement	Driving Wheel Diameter	Cylinder Bore × Stroke	Boiler Pressure	Notes
1918–29	0-6-0T	760 mm	240 × 380 mm	10 bar	ZOJE 1 -5 new to Zittau company
1903, 1909	0-4-4-0T	813 mm	215 × 355 mm (four cyls)	10 bar	Fairlee type
1924	0-6-6-0T	760 mm	240 × 380 mm	10 bar	
Reverted to original two locos 1916	0-6-6-0T	760 mm	240 × 380 mm	10 bar	
1925/26	0-6-2T	855 mm	324 × 400 mm	10 bar	Klose system
1925/26	0-6-2T	855 mm	324 × 400 mm	10 bar	Klose system
1930s–	0-4-4-0T	760 mm	HP 240 × 400 mm LP 370–400 × 400 mm	12/15 bar	Gunther Meyer type, compound
1934–42	0-8-0T	855 mm	HP 340 × 430 mm LP 530 × 430 mm	14 bar	Klien Lindner axles, compound
1969	0-10-0T	800 mm	430 × 400 mm	14 bar	
1974	0-10-0T	800 mm	430 × 400 mm	14 bar	
	2-10-2T	800 mm	450 × 400 mm	14 bar	Einheits standard design
	2-10-2T	800 mm	450 × 400 mm	14 bar	Neubau standard design

6

Other Narrow Gauge Railways

Narrow gauge railways have played an important role in the development of industries such as coal mining and forestry.

At Freital, the Zauckerode coal mine of the Royal Saxon Coal Company introduced the first electric mine railway in 1882, the same year that the first stage of the nearby Weisseritztalbahn was opened. It was built by Siemens & Halske only one year after Siemens had demonstrated the world's first electric tramway at Berlin.

Mine railways were very often of a temporary nature, particularly in opencast operations where tracks could be laid to serve the specific area being worked, and then later removed. Some fairly extensive systems developed, for example the brown coal or lignite workings at Olbersdorf near Zittau, and the Altenburger Land, a region south of Leipzig. In the Altenburg region the mines were developed from 1942, with a 900-mm-gauge system, which actually extended into the neighbouring state of Thuringia. Known as the Kammerforstbahn, it was used to transport the mined coal to nearby briquette manufacturing works at Haselbach and Regis Breitingen. The system was originally steam-operated, but later converted to overhead electric operation. The electric locomotives were built by LEW Henningsdorf to a standard low height, crocodile design, Class EL3, during the GDR period. Between 1951 and 1978 over 600 were built for use throughout East Germany. At its height the network was over 50 kilometres in length, and although coal mining remained an important industry throughout the GDR period, the industry was in severe and rapid decline following reunification, and the entire operation was closed in the mid-1990s.

In northern Saxony, in the region of Bad Muskau and Weisswasser, a local landowner and nobleman Count Hermann von Arnim sought to exploit the forest and coal resources in the area. The first section of 600-mm-gauge railway network was built in 1895, which at its peak had developed into a network some 80 kilometres in length. Railway routes were adapted and removed or replaced as required, and cargo carried included coal, wooden pit props, timber for paper mills and clay. After the First World War, the convenient choice of gauge allowed the railway to buy additional locomotives, rolling stock and other equipment which had been used by the army's field railways but was now surplus.

In 1901, the German army sought to develop a new design of locomotive for its field railways. The first engine was built by Henschel in 1903 although the firms Arnold

Above: At Olbersdorf opencast mine, close to Zittau, a Bo-Bo electric locomotive 4-177 sprouts pantographs in all directions, April 1991. (Neil Knowlden)

Below: A train of five side-tipping wagons at Olbersdorf. (Neil Knowlden)

Jüng and Krauss had also worked on the project. The design was an outside-framed eight-coupled side tank with 600-mm-diameter driving wheels, outside cylinders and Stephenson motion. Capable of hauling 70 tons, they were known as the Heeresfeldbahn Brigadelokomotive, and over 2,500 were built by a variety of manufacturers between 1914 and 1919. Originally designed and built with Klein Lindner axles to improve their flexibility on sharp curves, they were prone to derail, and this inconvenience, together with high maintenance requirements, led many to be rebuilt with conventional axles. Although they were scattered far and wide during the war, there was still a plentiful supply available in the years following. The Bad Muskau concern bought its first example in 1921, quickly followed by several more. At least eight were acquired over the next thirty years, one or two having worked as far away as Latvia, and used, often with four-wheel tenders, until their withdrawal between 1974 and 1978. All eight are preserved, with two still at Bad Muskau.

The railway and surrounding area was badly damaged in the Second World War, but such was the importance of the network, known as the Graf Arminsche Kleinbahn, that it was taken into the Deutsche Reichsbahn network. Although in the mid-1960s a review was conducted into the efficiency of the railway, as late as 1966 a new extension was built to serve a clay pit at Mühlrose. Increasingly, traffic was lost to lorries, and within a few years the network was gradually truncated until only the line from the clay pit to the brickworks that it served was still in use. The brickworks closed in 1992, and since then part of the

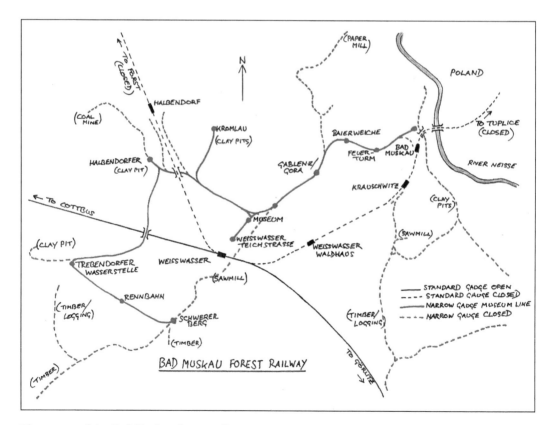

The extent of the Bad Muskau forest railway system.

Above: A museum train at Bad Muskau on the occasion of a charter by the author in August 2015. (Steve Dymott)

Below: No. 3312 waits to depart from Weisswasser in August 2015. (Steve Dymott)

railway has been reopened and developed as a heritage line. Ironically the last line built, to Mühlrose, was forced to close by the encroachment and expansion of the Nochten opencast coal mine. Although Weisswasser was at one time an important centre for glass production, and the heritage line operates partly in what is now a UNESCO World Heritage site, this part of the Upper Lusatia region, home of the ethnic Sorbs with their own Slavic language, has suffered economically since reunification, with high levels of unemployment.

One or two other industrial lines have been preserved in part, including a 3-kilometre stretch at Glossen, a station on the surviving Döllnitzbahn, which once served a quartzite quarry.

The Kirnitzschtalbahn, a rural tramway that runs from Bad Schandau on the banks of the River Elbe to Lichtenhain Waterfall, is included here as in many respects it was built to serve its community in a similar way to the narrow gauge railways. The first proposal was in 1893 for a line from Bad Schandau to Rainwiese, a town that is now Mezni Louka across the border in the Czech Republic. Bad Schandau had developed as a resort with the introduction of regular steamer services along the Elbe from Dresden, and the tramway was planned to provide another scenic tourist route into 'Saxon Switzerland'.

Only the 5-mile route from Bad Schandau to Lichtenhain Waterfall was built, to metre gauge, and running along the road, with the official opening on 28 May 1898. The first tram disgraced itself with a derailment, but the tramway was an immediate success, although only operated between May and October.

Initial thoughts of steam operation were soon abandoned and the tramway used 600 v DC overhead electric operation from the outset. A generating station was built at Bad Schandau, which within a few years was also supplying power to several other local communities. A fleet of twelve cars (six motor and six trailer) was built by the firm of Busch in Bautzen.

Disaster struck in July 1927 when a major fire destroyed the depot and the whole fleet. Within a few weeks replacement cars were obtained from the Lössnitz Tramway, which ran between Dresden and Radebeul. (The Lössnitz tramway was later converted to standard gauge and is now part of the Dresden city network.) New cars were obtained for the following year.

The original terminus in Bad Schandau was located in the town centre, but increasing traffic congestion resulted in a new terminus being opened in 1969, in the town's park, with the final 300 metres or so being abandoned.

Following the closure of the Lockwitztalbahn, which operated in a Dresden suburb until 1977, five of its trams were acquired, and over the following years more second-hand units arrived from Erfurt and Gotha. These still provide the regular service, although the company retains one of the 1928 cars, and a former Lockwitz car for private charter.

The tramway has been severely damaged by flooding on various occasions during its existence, most recently in 2002 and 2010, the reconstruction and remedial work lasting many months on each occasion.

In recent years the operator has installed an array of solar panels on the depot roof which enable it to meet all its power requirements on sunny summer days.

The Lockwitztalbahn mentioned above was a 9-kilometre-long interurban tramway linking Kreischa and Niedersedlitz along the Lockwitz Valley, south-east of Dresden, which was originally intended as an electric railway, promoted privately in 1895 by the

A tram leaves Lichtenhainer Waterfall for Bad Schandau in 1910.

Two heritage cars of the Kirnitzschtalbahn wait at the Bad Schandau terminus for a private charter, August 2015. The nearer car was acquired from the Lockwitztalbahn and carries the Niedersedlitz destination board. (Steve Dymott)

Daily services are operated by vehicles formerly used in Gotha and Erfurt. A three-car formation waits at Lichtenhainer Waterfall. (Steve Dymott)

engineer and entrepreneur Oskar Ludwig Kummer. Having obtained authority to build the line, Kummer's company was bankrupted in 1901 before work had started. Seven local authorities joined forces to petition the state for the line, initially unsuccessfully, but work commenced in 1905 with the line open to traffic the following March. In addition to passenger traffic, the cars also carried post, and a post office was built alongside the depot at Kreischa. Freight traffic was also carried during the First World War, but by the early 1920s the company was in a parlous financial situation, and closure was considered. The local Dresden tramway company DRÜVEG provided a loan, but was forced to take over the concern in 1929 when that could not be repaid. Improvements were made, but faced with increasing competition from buses, traffic declined during the 1930s, picking up again following the outbreak of war. The operation passed to Dresden Tramways with its takeover of DRÜVEG in 1941. The line did not escape the conflict unscathed, suffering bomb damage at Lockwitz in February 1945. Traffic levels increased post-war with new development in the area, and cars were refurbished in the early 1950s. A traffic study in 1956 recorded around 2,400 daily passengers, with excursion as well as local passengers. In the 1960s eight trams were brought in from Erfurt, but by then passenger numbers were falling, and this inevitable decline coupled with increasing traffic congestion led to a decision in 1974 to close the operation, with the final journey on 18 December 1977. Since reunification there have been attempts to establish a museum, and for a time one of the former Erfurt cars was displayed at Kreischa. This idea has now been abandoned, but

The last day of operation of the Lockwitztalbahn, 18 December 1977, with car Nos 240, 101 and 9.

sections of the route can still be easily traced with some track still in situ, and one of the postal vans is displayed in the Dresden Tram Museum.

All the narrow gauge lines built by the Saxon State Railways described in earlier chapters were of 750 mm gauge, but there were two exceptions built to metre gauge – both in the south-western Vogtland region. The first was a line 5 kilometres in length and built primarily for freight traffic between Reichenbach and Oberheinsdorf. Much of the route through Reichenbach involved street running, and when work started in 1901, several roads had to be widened to accommodate the railway. Much of the freight traffic was carried in standard gauge wagons, and the line became known as the Rollbockbahn. Passenger trains were added from 1909 as a result of local public pressure, which continued until 1957. By the early 1930s the railway had lost several important industrial customers, and the gradual decline in traffic, coupled with increasing traffic congestion led to complete closure in 1962. For the opening in 1902, three double-ended Fairlee-type locomotives were ordered from Hartmann, or Sächsische Maschinenfabrik as it had become. Originally numbered 251–53, with the later Reichsbahn system, they became 99 161–63. In 1943, No. 163 was requisitioned for war use, but was lost while aboard a ship in the Black Sea. The other two locomotives remained until closure, and fortunately 162 is now preserved in a small museum at Oberheinsdorf.

The second metre gauge line was an electrified route, which was always regarded as a narrow gauge railway although worked tramway style: the Klingenthalbahn, which linked Klingenthal with Sachsenberg and Georgenthal. After many years of discussion, and delays caused by the outbreak of the First World War, the 4-kilometre line, with a branch to the main

The last surviving double-ended Fairlie-type locomotive of the metre gauge Rollbockbahn is preserved at Oberheinsdorf. (Steve Dymott)

goods yard in Klingenthal, was finally built by Saxon State Railways and opened in 1916. However, although two electric locomotives had already been built, the overhead installation was not complete, as the military authorities would not release the copper required, and a steam locomotive had to be borrowed from the nearby Reichenbach–Oberheinsdorf line. The electrical installation was ready the following year, and the two locomotives were used for freight workings, with tramcar style vehicles for the passenger service.

In 1939, four tram cars were transferred from Austria, which had been annexed the previous year. The passenger cars were replaced in the 1950s, with the system voltage altered from 650 to 600 v DC, and when a new ski jump was built near Georgenthal in 1959 the line enjoyed an upsurge in traffic. By now the track and overhead wiring was worn out, and in urgent need of replacement. Some suitable replacement rail was sourced from the Soviet Union, but a length of only about 300 metres was actually replaced. Increasing concerns over traffic congestion with street running in the town centre at Klingenthal resulted in the abandonment of services in April 1964. The two freight locomotives remained until 1967, when they were sent to Dessau for scrap, but one tram car survives at Naumburg, and a freight wagon has been privately preserved.

Once other line is worth a mention: a long forgotten short metre gauge, freight-only route, just 1 kilometre long – the Deubener Güterbahn. This overhead electric line, authorised and built as a railway by the state operator, utilised two locomotives which, when built by Henschel in 1905 were the first electric locomotives owned by Saxon State Railways, although the actual operation of the line was handed over to Dresden tramways. The line was built purely to serve industry in the Freital Potschappel/Hainsberg area, which it continued to do until closure in 1972. One locomotive is preserved in the Dresden Tram Museum, while the other is exhibited in a museum at Kassel.

In addition to conventional narrow gauge lines, Saxony also has two metre gauge funicular railways, or *standseilbahnen.*

Around 15 kilometres south-east of Chemnitz, in the valley of the Zschopau river, the town of Erdmannsdorf is the lower terminus of the funicular that serves Augustusburg, a little town dominated by a castle and once a favourite hunting lodge of the Elector Augustus of Saxony. The first proposals for a line were put forward in 1897, but it was not until 24 June 1911 that the 1.2-kilometre line was opened. It has a maximum gradient of 20 per cent and a total rise in height of 168 metres. Like many such systems it operates two counterbalanced cars, with a passing point mid-way. The winding house is electrically powered.

The tough economic climate following the First World War forced the line to close for some months in 1923, but it reopened and in 1928 the cars were replaced. A major reconstruction took place between 1971 and 1973, with new cars supplied by a Hungarian builder. After reunification, the funicular became part of the Deutsche Bahn network for a time, and following another reconstruction in 2006 it is now operated by the regional transport authority, Verkehrsverbund Mittelsachsen. Each year since 2006 the company has

Dresden tram museum is the home of this diminutive overhead electric locomotive from the freight-only Deubener Güterbahn. (Steve Dymott)

promoted a race, 'man against machine', with runners competing against the eight-minute journey time of the railway!

The second funicular is to be found in the city of Dresden itself, running from the Loschwitz area to the Weisser Hirsch. The idea of the railway was first discussed in 1873, but over two decades elapsed before the line was finally opened on 25 September 1895. Although the line is only 547 metres long, it rises 94 metres with a maximum gradient of 29 per cent. For such a short line, it has an interesting structure, with two tunnels and a viaduct en route. It is essentially single line, with a crossing on the viaduct section. Originally the winding gear was steam-operated, but this was converted to electricity in 1908. The first cars were retired in 1934, with their replacements operating until 1962, and one of the latter is now preserved in the city's transport museum. The lower terminus station was destroyed in the Second World War, during the attack of 13 February 1945, but the cars had been stored in the tunnels and were undamaged. The line has been refurbished on several more occasions since, most recently in 2014, and operates as an integral part of the city's transport network.

Nearby is another funicular railway, although strictly not a narrow gauge line as it is a suspended monorail. The Schwebebahn links Loschwitz with Oberloschwitz, and dates from 1901. It is 274 metres long, with a gradient of 39 per cent, and operates with two cars, one suspended from each side of the structure. From 1984 until 1992 it was out of commission, but remains in regular service, run by the city tram and bus operator.

It may also be appropriate to mention that temporary narrow gauge lines, known as *trümmerbahnen*, or rubble railways, were extensively used in clearing debris from the

A general view of the Dresden–Loschwitz funicular railway, *c.* 1900.

The Weisser Hirsch upper terminus, August 2005.

centre of both Leipzig and Dresden following the terrible destruction caused by the Second World War. In Leipzig there were actually three separate networks, mainly laid to 600-mm gauge, and in 1946 one system alone was operating a fleet of no less than sixteen steam and twelve diesel locomotives with nearly 600 tipper wagons. Initially set up by contractors the operations were later taken over by municipal authorities. Track layouts were altered as the work progressed, and they continued in use until as late as 1955.

Between 1927 and 1929 another temporary railway, about 8 kilometres in length, was in operation between Wilsdruff and the construction site of the Niederwartha dam and pumped storage scheme.

The concept of a miniature park railway largely operated by children first appeared in the Soviet Union in 1932, and in the post Second World War era extended to other eastern bloc countries. These Pioneer or Children's railways were designed to train youngsters in the disciplines of railway operation – a principle still employed today.

Longest of the children's railways is the Dresdner Parkeisenbahn opened in the war-torn city's Grosser Garten in 1950. It has a total length of five kilometres, partly double track, built to

The Dresden Schwebebahn is a monorail rather than a narrow gauge railway, but is nevertheless worthy of inclusion. A car at the upper terminus in 1994.

381-mm (15-inch) gauge and with miniature locomotives, based on standard-gauge prototypes, closely modelled on the UK's Ravenglass & Eskdale Railway. The railway is largely operated by children between the ages of eight and sixteen, although with adult train drivers, and others very much in the background. When built, it was only intended to stay for one season, but such was its success that it was extended, and now carries some 250,000 passengers annually.

The second Pioniereisenbahn to open in the GDR in 1951 can be found in Leipzig. It is also 381-mm gauge and has a length of 2 kilometres circling a lake, the Auensee, which was formed from a gravel pit.

Two other lines, at Chemnitz and Görlitz, are 600-mm gauge, and that at Görlitz often uses a locomotive based on the 1837 prototype *Adler*, with appropriately styled carriages, while Chemnitz uses industrial narrow gauge motive power, both steam and diesel.

Saxony has a rich narrow gauge heritage, not only with the story of the state sponsored railways and mini networks, but a fascinating variety of other light railways, both passenger and industrial. With several lines still in everyday commercial operation, still steam worked, and others established as volunteer run museum railways, it is certainly an area worth exploring. Well into the twenty-first century it is still possible to find two narrow gauge railways, each with a daily steam service, close to a major European city. In addition, the routes of many of the long closed lines can still be traced quite easily, with much of their infrastructure still extant. While we are familiar with the idea of miniature railways in the UK, we have no history of the children's railway concept, and it is interesting to watch and study the way in which they are run. The industrial landscape has changed dramatically in the years since the reunification of Germany, with the consequent loss of mining and other private railways, but the passenger lines are now regarded as an integral part of the local economy, and extensively promoted for their value to tourism.

Above: Battery electric locomotive EA01 dates from 1962, seen here at the main terminus of the Dresden park railway. (Steve Dymott)

Below: Pacific 03-002 of the Leipzig park railway dates from 1925.

Dienstmasse
Lok u. Tender
Wasser   8.1 t
Kohle   0,9 m
Bremsbauart   0,2 t
Bremsmasse   K-mZ
                P11 t
Br.1 16.11.18

Above: A replica of the Stephenson-built *Adler* regularly operates at the park railway in Görlitz. (R. Dietrich)

Left: Taking water at the rebuilt Weisseritztalbahn shortly after reopening to Dippoldiswalde in December 2008. (Steve Dymott)

Appendix

Railways and Museums to Visit

Daily Operation

Weisseritztalbahn, Freital-Hainsberg–Kurort Kipsdorf, www.weisseritztalbahn.de

Lossnitzgrundbahn, Radebeul Ost–Radeburg, www.lossnitzgrundbahn.de

Fichtelbergbahn, Cranzahl–Oberwiesenthal, www.fichtelbergbahn.de

Döllnitzbahn, Oschatz–Mugeln–Glossen/Kemmlitz, www.doellnitzbahn.de

Zittauer Schmalspurbahnen, Zittau–Kurort Jonsdorf and Kurort Oybin, www.zittauer-schmalspurbahn.de

Kirnitzschtalbahn, rural tramway, Bad Schandau–Lichtenhein Waterfall, www.ovps.de

Museum Railways

Pressnitztalbahn, Steinbach – Johstadt, www.pressnitztalbahn.de

Museumsbahn Schönheide, Stutzengrun Neulehn – Schönheide, www.museumsbahn-schoenheide.de

Saechsisches Schmalspurbahn Museum, Bahnhof Oberrittersgrün, www.schmalspurmuseum.de

Schwarzbachbahn, Bahnhof Lohsdorf, www.schwarzbachbahn.de

Waldeisenbahn Muskau, Weisswasser–Kromlau/Krauschwitz–Bad Muskau, www.waldeisenbahn.de

Coal railway, Meuselwitz–Regis Breitingen, www.kohlebahnen.de

Railway Museum, Oberheinsdorf, www.oberheinsdorfergrund-vogtland.de

Wilsdruff Station Museum, Wilsdruff, www.wilsdruffer-schmalspurnetz.de

Dresden Transport Museum, Neumarkt, Dresden, www.verkehrsmuseum-dresden.de

Quarry Railway, Glossen, www.feldbahn-glossen.de

Park Railways

Dresden, Grosser Garten, www.parkeisenbahn-dresden.de

Chemnitz, www.parkeisenbahn-chemnitz.de

Leipzig, www.parkeisenbahn-auensee-leipzig.de

Gorlitz, www.goerlitzerparkeisenbahn.de

Bibliography

Brendel, Martin, André Marks and Wolfram Wagner, *Die Lokomotiven der Sächsischen Schmalspurbahnen,* Volumes 1–3 (SSB Medien, 2018/19)

Hans-Jürgen, Knabe, *Museum Rittersgrün: Sächsisches Schmalspurbahn-Museum Rittersgrün* (Deutscher Kunstverlag, 2000)

Kirsche, Hans-Joachim, *Bahnland DDR* (Berlin: VEB Verlag für Verkehrswesen, 1990)

Lenhard, Dirk, Moll Gerhard and Scheffler Reiner, *Die sächsische IV K. Die Reichsbahn-Baureihe 99 51-60* (EK Verlag, 2004)

Organ, John, *Saxony and Baltic Germany Revisited* (Middleton Press, 2015)

Preus, Reiner, *Alles über Schmalspurbahnen in Sachsen* (Stuttgart: transpress, 2009)

Rainer, Heinrich, *Die Klingenthaler Schmalspurbahn und die Geschichte des Normalspurbahnhofs Klingenthal* (Ausgabe 2 Verlag, Kenning, Nordhorn, 2000)

Rettig, Wilfried, *Die DR Schmalspurbahnen 1965–1990* (EK Verlag, 2018)

Vetter, Klaus-Jürgen, *Das war die Deutsche Reichsbahn* (München: GeraMond, 2019)

Eisenbahn Atlas Deutschland (Schweers & Wall, 2007)

Wolf, Karl and Ludger Kenning, *Wilkau–Hasslau–Carlsfeld. Die erste und längste Sächsischen Schmalspurbahn* (Kenning Verlag, 1996)

Wolfram, Wagner and Reiner Scheffler, *Die II K (alt), III K und V K, sowie Fremdlokomotiven auf Sächsischen Schmalspurbahnen* (Egglham Bufe – Fachbuchverlag, 1996)

Acknowledgements

I would like to thank all those both in the UK and Germany who have assisted with information and illustrations. In particular, I would like to mention Steve Dymott, Neil Knowlden and Ed Kaas for allowing me to use their photographic collections so freely. Further, many of Neil's pictures would not have been possible without transport provided by John Graham. In Germany, to Achim Rickelt, plus friends at Schmalspurbahnmuseum Rittersgrün, Schwarzbachbahn and Traditionsbahn Radebeul – *vielen Dank!*

Finally thanks to Roger MacDonald for putting up with many requests to trawl his library, for reading through my script, offering advice and corrections – particularly relating to German grammar!